Publisher: DA Properties

© DA Properties (UK) Ltd

ISBN 978-0-9935584-9-8

All brand names, trademarks and products referenced in this book are owned by their respective owners. No affiliation or payments have been received by companies in this publication and they have not endorsed this book.

Limit of Liability/Disclaimer of Warranty: While every effort has been made by the author and publisher to their best efforts to represent information correctly they make no representation or warranties with respect to the accuracy or completeness of the contents of this book and disclaim any implied warranties for any particular purpose. Neither the publisher or the author is responsible for offering any professional advice and that expert advice should be sought before acting on the information contained within.

THE BRIDGE FOR HEROES

The Bridge for Heroes is a small charity that exists to support members of the Armed Forces Community in and around West Norfolk by providing support, information, advice and guidance for those lost and confused, companionship and activities for the lonely and isolated, nourishment for the thirsty and hungry, shelter for the homeless, release to those who feel imprisoned, and a safe haven for all.

The Charity was set up in 2010 by Mike Taylor, with support from a small team of individuals, who were concerned about the long term effect on the mental health and wellbeing of some of our HM Armed Force Community. Mike's own experiences convinced him that improved provision and understanding of mental health support, specifically catering for the needs of serving and ex-serving personnel and their families, was vital in helping those who were struggling to cope in 'civvy' street and subsequently saving lives.

Since its start, mental health awareness has increased immensely in the public eye, allowing the Charity to make steady progress, provide swift interventions and address individuals needs holistically, with on-going and long-term support. This support is now proactively achieved through one to one sessions, innovative group therapies, activities and local community events.

Furthermore, the Charity signposts individuals to specialist services that cater for their specific needs and works in close partnership with other organisations, agencies and charities who are able to assist in specific areas that can affect the Armed Forces Community when they finish their service and return to civilian life. It is worth noting that some problems, particularly in the areas of mental health, may not reveal themselves until several years after the person has left the services.

The Bridge for Heroes main areas of charitable activity are the provision of help and support through talk therapy sessions, information, guidance, advice, respite, activities, refreshments and light lunches.

The Charity's holistic approach means that whatever the issue, its staff and volunteers will always be there to help and support our local Armed Forces Community.

For current information take a look at the website www.thebridgeforheroes.org

This cookbook has been put together by Jim Grant and other people who support The Bridge for Heroes. We would like to thank everyone for their time and support.

All recipes are designed for 4 people unless stated otherwise

Proceeds from the sale of this book will go towards the much-needed outreach programme that The Bridge for Heroes charity runs.

CONTENT

Measurements

oz.	gm
⅛	3.5
¼	7
⅓	9
½	14
⅔	19
¾	21
1	28
2	57
3	85
4	110
5	140
6	170
7	200
8	225
9	255
10	280
11	310

pt	ml
⅛	70
¼	140
½	280
¾	430
1	570
2	1140
4	2270

fl oz.	ml
2	60
5	150
8	250
10	300

cup	
1 cup	250

inch	cm
¼	0.6
½	1.3
1	2.5
1 ½	4
2	5
2 ½	6.3
3	7.6
4	10.2
5	12.7
6	15.2
6 ½	16.5
7	17.8
12	30.5
18	45.7

abbreviations	
tsp	tea spoon
tbsp.	table spoon
lb	pound
oz.	ounce
ltr.	litre
fl oz.	fluid ounce
pt.	pint
gm	gram
ml	millilitre
cup	cup
min	minutes
hr	hours

Oven Temperatures

	C	GAS	F
SLOW (COOL)	110	¼	225
	130	½	250
	140	1	275
	150	2	300
	160	3	325
MODERATE	180	4	350
	190	5	375
	200	6	400
HOT	220	7	425
	230	8	450
VERY HOT	240	9	475

Food for thought

Like every other organ in the body, our brains need nutrition to survive and thrive in the day-to-day functioning. The cliché that a healthy body means a healthy mind came to light based on fact: keeping a balanced and healthy diet can have a direct, positive effect on mental health and wellbeing. This survival guide aims at providing hearty, nutritional and easy-to-follow recipes to keep a healthy body, combined with mindfulness tips and quotes to keep a healthy mind.

Soups

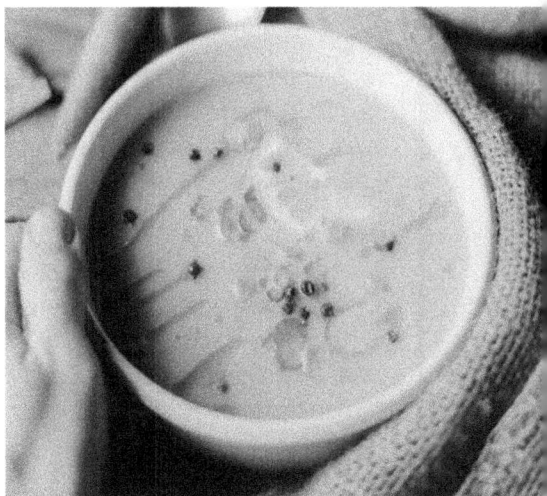

" Heroism doesn't always happen in a burst of glory. Sometimes small triumphs and large hearts change the course of history."- Mary Roach

Mindful eating

Know when you are full. Eating past the point of being full can affect the nutritional balance in your body. An imbalanced body can lead to an imbalanced brain and become detrimental to your mental health.

Know when you are hungry. Eating when our bodies tell us to is the prime time for nutritional uptake. Stomach growls, feeling groggy and lacking energy are tell-tale signs of hunger so eat in sync with your body's needs.

Social eating. Isolation is known for having negative effects on mental health so only eating alone can develop the same negative feelings. Eating with others stimulates your brain while socialising. If you cannot have guests, or be a guest, calling or video-calling friends or family can be an alternative.

Structured eating. Allocating a set amount of time each day to prepare and eat food is important for digestive regulation. Eating in a specific place is key too, in order to stimulate the digestive system. These also contribute to mindfulness in routine thinking, de-cluttering your mind and breaking down the day offering respite and relief for daily activities.

Eating foods that are healthy and nutritionally valuable. Like every other organ in the body, our brains need nutrition to survive and thrive in the day-to-day functioning. Healthy body, healthy mind.

When eating, focus on eating alone. Multitasking while eating does not give your brain time to process the activity, therefore no stimulation for the digestive system. Focus on chewing food and appreciating the work gone into preparing it. Focus on where it came from and appreciate the break. Food is fuel for our power and so sitting and absorbing that power is much easier to do when you aren't multitasking and using the that fuel straight away.

CHICKEN SOUP

Ingredients

- ❖ 4 oz. onion, leek and celery
- ❖ 2 oz. butter or margarine
- ❖ 2 oz. flour
- ❖ 2 pt. chicken stock
- ❖ bouquet garni
- ❖ salt and pepper
- ❖ ½ pt. milk or ¼ pt. cream
- ❖ 1 oz. diced chicken (garnish)

Method

1 Gently cook the sliced onion, leek and celery in the butter or margarine without colouring
2 Mix in the flour, cook over a gentle heat to a sandy texture without colouring
3 Cool slightly, gradually mix in the hot stock, stir to the boil
4 Add the bouquet garni and season
5 Simmer for 30 -40 min, skim as necessary
6 Remove the bouquet garni
7 Liquidise or pass through a fine strainer
8 Return to the pan, re-boil and finish with milk or cream, correct the seasoning
9 Add the garnish and serve
   Note: - chicken stock cubes can be used as stock

LEEK AND POTATO SOUP

Ingredients

- ❖ 1 lb leeks trimmed and washed
- ❖ 1 oz. butter or margarine
- ❖ 1 ½ pt. white stock
- ❖ bouquet garni
- ❖ 8 oz. potatoes
- ❖ salt and pepper

Method

1 Cut the white and light green of the leek into ¼ inch paysanne
2 Slowly cook in the butter in a pan with a lid on until soft but without colouring
3 Add the stock, the bouquet garni, potatoes diced into ¼ inch cubes,
season with salt and pepper
4 Simmer until the leeks and potatoes are cooked approx. 20 min,
Then remove the bouquet garni
Note: - soup can be enriched by adding 1–2 oz. butter and ⅛ pt. cream.
Also if required smooth liquidised or passed through a fine strainer

MIXED VEGETABLE SOUP

<u>Ingredients</u>

* ❖ 12 oz. mixed vegetables
* ❖ Onions, leeks, carrots, turnips, cabbage and celery
* ❖ 2 oz. butter or margarine
* ❖ 1 ½ pt. white stock (chicken)
* ❖ bouquet garni
* ❖ salt and pepper
* ❖ 1 oz. peas
* ❖ 1 oz. French beans

<u>Method</u>

1 Cut the peeled, washed vegetables into paysanne. Thinly cut into ½ inch squares or triangles
2 Cook slowly in butter in a pan cover until tender, do not colour
3 Add the hot stock, bouquet garni, season and simmer for approx. 20-30 min
4 Add the peas and beans, simmer until all vegetables are cooked
5 Skim off all fat, add salt and pepper to taste and serve

Note: - for autumn vegetable soup use
  4 oz. courgettes
  4 oz. red, yellow and green peppers
  4 oz. potatoes
  4 oz. celery
  4 oz. onions
  2 oz. butter or margarine
  ½ pt. vegetable stock
  salt and pepper
  bouquet garni

MUSHROOM SOUP

<u>Ingredients</u>

* ❖ 4 oz. onion, leek and celery
* ❖ 2 oz. butter or margarine
* ❖ 2 oz. flour
* ❖ 2 pt. white stock. (chicken)
* ❖ 8 oz. white mushrooms
* ❖ Bouquet garni
* ❖ Salt and pepper
* ❖ ¼ pt. milk

<u>Method</u>

1 Gently cook the sliced onions, leeks and celery in the butter or margarine in a pan without colouring
2 Mix in the flour, cook over a gentle heat to a sandy texture without colouring
3 Gradually mix in the hot stock. Stir to the boil, add the well washed, chopped mushrooms, bouquet garni and season
4 Simmer for 30–40 min, skim as necessary
5 Remove the bouquet garni, liquidise or pass through a medium strainer
6 Return to a clean pan, re-boil, add salt and pepper to taste and for consistency add milk or cream
   Note: - natural yoghurt, skimmed milk or non-dairy cream may be added in place of dairy cream

SQUASH SOUP

Ingredients

- ❖ 1 small squash
- ❖ 1 medium potato
- ❖ 1 onion
- ❖ vegetable oil
- ❖ salt and pepper
- ❖ 1 tsp ground garlic
- ❖ ¼ tsp ground ginger
- ❖ 1 pt. vegetable stock

Method

1. Skin and dice the squash and potato
2. Peel the onion and finely dice
3. Place the onions in a pan with the oil and cook, do not colour
4. Add the diced squash and potato
5. Add the vegetable stock, salt, pepper, garlic and ginger
6. Bring to the boil and simmer for 30–45 min, skim as necessary
7. Liquidise or pass through a fine strainer
8. Return to the pan and add salt and pepper to taste
   Note: - milk or cream can be added if required

Meat

Dishes

"We sleep peaceably in our beds at night only because rough men stand ready to do violence on our behalf."- George Orwell

Hydration station

Drinking 6-8 cups of water keeps your body hydrated and therefore your mind.

Drinking more water can improve memory, reduce headaches and leave you better able to concentrate throughout the day.

Try new things

Experimenting with new things such as trying a new food or activity keep the mind active and stimulated.

Even if you don't enjoy the new introduction, your mental health will benefit from the change and encourage you to keep trying new things in the future.

COLA GAMMON

Ingredients

- ❖ Gammon Joint
- ❖ 2 ltr full sugar cola (DO NOT USE DIET)
- ❖ 2 red onions, peeled and quartered
- ❖ onion gravy granules

Method

Meat
1. Take the gammon joint and lightly wash with clean water.
2. Place the gammon join in a slow cooker or in a large ovenproof pot, skin side down
3. Surround the meat with the onions and cover with the cola
4. Season with a generous grind of salt and pepper
5. Cook on a medium heat, medium setting on a slow cooker or 80C in the oven, for 8 hours
6. After 8 hours, remove the joint and place in a roasting tray, skin side up
7. Cut any strings and carefully peel the top layer of skin off, exposing the fatty layer
8. With a knife, score diamonds into the fat and season with salt and pepper again and use a ladle (6-8 tablespoons) of the cola to glaze
9. Roast in the oven, with the onions from the liquid, at 200C for 20 minutes or until the fat is crisp
10. Once crisp, remove from the oven and use forks to pull the meat apart

Sauce
1. In a small saucepan, pour the desired amount of liquid for your sauce with a few of the leftover onions
2. Whilst the meat is roasting, bring the liquid to the boil and let simmer until the meat is ready for serving
3. Once ready, stir in onion gravy until desired consistency

Serve with roasted root vegetables and boiled, tender stem broccoli

IRISH STEW

Ingredients

- 1 ¼ lb stewing lamb
- bouquet garni
- 1 lb potatoes
- 4 oz. onions
- 4 oz. celery
- 4 oz. savoy cabbage
- 4 oz. leeks
- 4 oz. button onions
- 4 oz. chopped parsley

Method

1. Trim the meat and cut into even pieces, blanch and refresh
2. Place in a shallow saucepan, cover with water, bring to the boil season with salt and skim. If tough meat is being used Allow ½ to 1 hour stewing before adding any vegetables
3. Add the bouquet garni, turn the potatoes into barrel shape
4. Cut the potato trimmings, onions, celery, cabbage and leeks into small neat pieces and add to the meat, simmer for 30 min
5. Add the button onions and simmer for further 30 min
6. Add the potatoes and simmer gently, with the lid on the pan until cooked
7. Add salt and pepper to taste and skim off the fat, remove bouquet garni
   Serve with a sprinkling of chopped parsley

SAUSAGE TOAD IN THE HOLE

Ingredients

- ❖ 8 sausages of choice
- ❖ Yorkshire pudding mix
- ❖ 4 oz. flour
- ❖ salt
- ❖ 1 egg
- ❖ ½ pt. milk
- ❖ 1 oz. oil or dripping

Method (Yorkshire pudding)

1. Sieve the flour and salt into a basin and make a well in the centre
2. Break the egg, add half the liquid and whisk to a smooth mixture
3. Gradually adding the rest of the liquid and allow to rest

Method   (Sausage toad in the hole)
1. Place the sausages in a roasting tin or oven proof dish with a little oil
2. Place in a hot oven at 230-250C for 5-10 min
3. Remove, add the Yorkshire pudding and return to the oven until the sausages and Yorkshire pudding are cooked, approx. 20 min
4. Cut into portions and serve with a thick gravy

SHEPHERDS PIE

Ingredients

- 4 oz. chopped onion
- 1 ½ oz. fat or oil
- 1 lb cooked lamb or mutton (minced)
- salt and pepper
- 2-3 drops of Worcester sauce
- ¼ to ½ pt. jus-lie/demi-glace
- 1 lb cooked potatoes
- 1 oz. margarine /milk

Method

1   Cook the onions in the fat or oil without colouring
2   Add the cooked meat from which all fat and gristle has been removed
3   Season, add the Worcester sauce and sufficient sauce to bind
4   Bring to boil, simmer for 10-15 min
5   Place in a pie or earthenware dish
6   Prepare the mashed potatoes and pipe or arrange neatly on top
7   Brush with milk or egg wash
8   Colour in hot oven or grill
9   Serve with sauce boat of jus-lie (lightly thickened meat juice)

Note: - substitute lamb for beef mince for cottage pie

SWEET AND SOUR PORK

Ingredients

* ❖ 10 oz. loin of pork
* ❖ ½ oz. sugar
* ❖ ⅛ pt. of sherry dry
* ❖ ⅛ pt. of soy sauce
* ❖ ⅛ pt. veg oil
* ❖ 2 oz. cornflour
* ❖ 2 tbsp. oil
* ❖ 2 clove of garlic
* ❖ 2 oz. fresh ginger
* ❖ 3 oz. chopped onion
* ❖ 1 green pepper diced to ½ in
* ❖ 2 chillies chopped
* ❖ ⅛ pt. sweet and sour sauce
* ❖ 2 pineapple rings
* ❖ 2 spring onions

Method

1. Cut the pork loin into ¼ in pieces
2. Marinade the pork for 30 min in the sugar, sherry and soy sauce
3. Pass the pork through the cornflour pressing the cornflour well
4. Deep fry the pork pieces in oil at 190C until golden brown
5. Add a tbsp. of oil to the pan, add the garlic and ginger, fry until fragrant
6. Add the onion, pepper and chillies, sauté for a few minutes
7. Stir in the sweet and sour sauce, bring to the boil
8. Add the pineapple, cut into small chunks, thicken slightly with diluted cornflour and simmer for 2 min
9. Deep fry the pork again until crisp, drain, mix into the vegetables and sauce
10. Serve with garnish of rings of spring onion

Fish

"It is foolish and wrong to mourn the men who died. Rather, we should thank God that such men lived."-George S. Patton Jr.

Square Breathing

Square breathing is a calming CBT technique useful when feeling anxious, stressed or overwhelmed. Take any 4-sided object and start in the top-left corner. Inhale for 4 counts while holding your finger on that corner. Exhale for 4 counts while travelling your finger to the top-right. Once at the top-right corner, inhale again for 4 counts and exhale while travelling your finger to the bottom-right corner. Repeat this process while travelling your finger around the shape. If, once the shape is completed, you feel this has not offered much relief, start again. This is a quick and easy technique to ground and self-soothe when you are struggling.

BEER-BATTERED FISH

Ingredients

- ❖ fish of choice (fillets skinned if you prefer)
- ❖ 180 gm plain flour
- ❖ 55 gm cornflour
- ❖ 1 tsp baking powder
- ❖ ¼ tsp fine salt
- ❖ 250ml golden ale
- ❖ 2 lemons 1 juiced (you need 2 tbsp.) 1 cut into wedges
- ❖ sunflower oil for deep frying

Method

1   Mix 150 gm of flour, cornflour, baking powder and salt into a bowl and make a well in the centre. Pour in the ale and 1½ tbsp. of lemon juice and whisk until batter is completely smooth and bubbly

2   Half fill a large saucepan with oil then heat to 180C use a thermometer to check the temperature. (If you do not have a thermometer then carefully dip the handle of a wooden spoon into the oil. If it is hot enough it should bubble steadily. If it bubbles vigorously it is too hot.)

4   Season the fish and dust in the remaining flour, using tongs dip the fish into the batter to coat, then lower into the hot oil.

5   Cook for 5-6 minutes turning until golden brown and crispy

6   Transfer to a wire rack over a tray to stop the fish going soggy and to catch any excess oil
Note: - the ale can be an Indian pale ale or a light bitter.
You can use a deep sided fry pan or a wok if required

COD FISHCAKES

Ingredients

- ❖ 8 oz. cooked, skinned and boned white fish (cod, haddock, etc.)
- ❖ 8 oz. mashed potatoes
- ❖ salt, pepper
- ❖ 1 oz. flour
- ❖ 2 eggs
- ❖ 2 oz. breadcrumbs

Method

1   Combine the fish, potatoes, 1 egg and season with salt and pepper
2   Divide into 4 equal pieces, mould into balls
3   Pass through the coating of flour, egg and breadcrumbs
4   Flatted slightly, neaten with a pallet knife   or large flat knife
5   Deep fry in hot fat (185C/365F) for 2 to 3 min, until golden brown
    Note: -   ask your fish monger to skin and bone the fish
        breadcrumbs can be made from 2 slices of bread or
    bought ready made

FISH PIE

Ingredients

- ❖ ½ pint béchamel sauce
- ❖ 8 oz. fish cooked free from skin and bones
- ❖ 2oz cooked dices mushrooms
- ❖ 1 chopped hardboiled egg
- ❖ 8 oz. mashed potatoes
- ❖ Salt, pepper, chopped parsley

Method

1. Bring the béchamel to the boil
2. Add the fish, mushrooms, egg and parsley. Add salt and pepper to taste
3. Place in a buttered pie dish
4. Place or pipe the potato on top, brush with egg wash or milk
5. Brown in a hot oven or under grill and serve

MEDITERRANEAN TUNA STEAKS

Ingredients

- ❖ 4 tuna steaks
- ❖ 1 cup green and black olives, halved
- ❖ 8 sundried tomatoes in sunflower oil, chopped into 1cm pieces
- ❖ 4 tablespoons of olive oil
- ❖ salt and black pepper to taste

Method

1. Preheat the oven to 180C/gas mark 4
2. Tear off 4 strips of tin foil, large enough to loosely fold around the tuna steaks
3. Place one tuna steak in the centre of the foil and turn up the edges of the foil to create a makeshift bowl.
4. To the tuna, add 1 table spoon of olive oil to coat the tuna.
5. Season the tuna with salt and pepper
6. Add 1 quarter of the halved olives and 1 quarter of the chopped sun dried tomatoes to the tuna
7. Loosely fold the tin foil around the tuna, leaving a small opening in the top, making a parcel
8. Repeat this process with each tuna steak and place the parcels on a deep baking tray
9. Bake in the preheated oven for 30 minutes or until the fish flakes with a fork.

Note: -remove the parcels carefully from the tray as the foil will be hot serving suggestion is with couscous and roasted Mediterranean vegetables

SALMON, SWEET CHILLI AND SWEET POTATO FISH CAKES

Ingredients (for 4 fishcakes)

- 400g salmon fillet
- large sweet potatoes (approx. 400g) peeled and chopped into 2 inch cubes
- 50ml semi-skimmed milk
- 50ml sweet chilli sauce any brand
- 1 large egg
- sieved flour for dusting
- 100g breadcrumbs, normal or panko

Method

1   Boil the potatoes in a large saucepan for 10 minutes with a pinch of salt.
2   Drain the potatoes well and place back on the heat for 2 minutes to evaporate the rest of the water and take off the heat
3   In a microwaveable bowl, put the salmon fillets, milk and sweet chilli sauce, cover and microwave on high for 2 minutes or until the fish is flaky and opaque.
4   In the microwavable bowl, add the sweet potato and blend with a spoon or hands.
5   Line a baking tray with greaseproof paper on 3 small pates, beat the egg on one, sprinkle the flour on one and place breadcrumbs on the third.
6   With hands, mould patties with the mixture, 2cm thick and palm sized. With each patty, coat in flour, then the egg mixture and finally coat with breadcrumbs
7   Place the fishcakes on the baking tray and place in the fridge for 1 hour to solidify shape.
8   When ready to cook, preheat oven to 200 degrees/gas mark 4 and bake for 25-30 minutes or until breadcrumbs are golden brown

Note: -   serve with long stem broccoli and chips
          Why not make your own breadcrumbs?
Take semi-stale bread, salt and pepper and mix in a blender until fine crumbs

Vegetarian

"Never give in, never give in, never, never, never, never—in nothing, great or small, large or petty—never give in except to convictions of honour and good sense."
– Winston Churchill

4-minute meditation

Meditation can seem pointless and be intimidating to begin, so let's start with 4 minutes. Find a quiet space, away from distractions and set a timer for 4 minutes. Close your eyes and sit in a relaxed position. Focus on your breathing naturally, how your body feels with each inhale and exhale. Which muscles move and how does each breath make your feel. If you become distracted of feel your mind start to wander, bring your focus back onto breathing. Soon enough the 4 minutes will be up and you will have taken a little time for yourself.

CHEESE AND ONION FLAN

Ingredients

- ❖ 1 large potatoes peeled and chopped into small pieces
- ❖ 1 medium onion sliced small
- ❖ 16 oz. hard cheese of choice (cheddar, cathedral etc.)
- ❖ 6 or 8-inch flan dish or bought savoury flan case
- ❖ 1 tomato
- ❖ 1 or 2 tsp of mustard

Method

1. Boil the potatoes
2. Cook the chopped onions in oil until soft but do not brown
3. Grate the cheese
4. Mix the potatoes, onions, cheese and mustard together until smooth
5. Empty the mix into your flan case and level off
6. Cook in oven 180c 30 to 35 min
7. For last 10 min decorate with grated cheese and sliced tomato

Note: - you can make the pastry following the instructions for short pastry you can use any mustard of choice

CHINESE STYLE STIR FRY VEGETABLES

Ingredients

- ❖ 4 oz. bean sprouts
- ❖ 4 oz. button mushrooms
- ❖ 4 oz. carrots
- ❖ 4 oz. celery
- ❖ 4 oz. cauliflower
- ❖ 4 oz. broccoli
- ❖ 2 oz. baby sweetcorn
- ❖ 2 oz. French beans
- ❖ 2 oz. red pepper
- ❖ 2 oz. green pepper
- ❖ ½ pt. sunflower oil
- ❖ ¼ oz. grated root ginger
- ❖ ⅛ pt. soy sauce

Method

1   Wash the bean sprouts, wash and slice the mushrooms, peel the carrots cut into batons, trim and cut celery into batons, wash the cauliflower and broccoli and cut into florets, top and tail the French beans and cut in half, wash and slice the peppers. The green vegetables may be blanched to retain their colour
2   Heat the oil in a wok or large deep frying pan and add the vegetables fry and continually stir for approx. 3 min
3   Add the grated ginger, cook for 1 min, add the soy sauce, stir well
4   Add salt and pepper to taste and serve straight away
    Note: - you can use any vegetables you like, substitute vegetables as required
    you can use ginger out of a jar if required 1 or 2 tsp to taste

DAIRY FREE VEGETABLE QUICHE

Ingredients

- ❖ 1 recipe pie crust or a store bought crust or go crust less
- ❖ 1tbsp olive oil
- ❖ 3 handfuls of baby spinach roughly chopped
- ❖ 1 small onion
- ❖ 1 red pepper diced
- ❖ 5-10 asparagus spear ends trimmed then chopped into 1 in pieces
- ❖ 6 eggs
- ❖ ¾ cup of unsweetened almond milk
- ❖ 3 tbsp. baking powder
- ❖ ½ tsp all-purpose flour
- ❖ ½ tsp salt
- ❖ ½ tsp sweet paprika
- ❖ ½ tsp dried thyme
- ❖ ¼ tsp chipotle powder
- ❖ ⅛ tsp black pepper

Method

1. Heat the oil and add the onion, chopped red pepper and asparagus and sauté for 5 min or until onions are translucent and asparagus is cooked
2. Remove from heat
3. In a separate bowl whisk the eggs, flour, baking powder, and almond milk, salt, paprika, thyme, chipotle powder and black pepper.
4. Stir in the sauté vegetables and fresh spinach and stir until well combined
5. Pour the egg and vegetable mixture into the pastry dish
6. Bake at 180C for 45 min or until a skewer inserted comes out clean
7. Remove from oven and allow to cool for 5 min
   Note: - you can substitute vegetables for any other that you like

MACARONI CHEESE

Ingredients

- ❖ 4 oz. macaroni
- ❖ 1 oz. butter (optional)
- ❖ 4 oz. grated cheese
- ❖ 1 pt. thin béchamel
- ❖ ½ tsp diluted mustard
- ❖ salt and pepper

Method

1. Plunge the macaroni into a pan of boiling water
2. Allow to boil gently and stir occasionally with a wooden spoon
3. Cook for approx. 15 min and drain well in a colander
4. Return to a clean pan containing the butter
5. Mix with half the cheese and the béchamel and mustard
6. Place in an earthen ware dish and sprinkle with the remaining cheese
7. Brown under the grill

Ingredients for Béchamel (white sauce)

- ❖ 4 oz. butter, margarine or oil (fat)
- ❖ 4 oz. flour
- ❖ 1 ½ pt. milk (as required for thickness)
- ❖ 1 studded onion

Method

1. Melt the fat in a sauce pan
2. Add the flour and mix in to a paste
3. Cook for a few min without colouring
4. Remove from heat and cool the roux
5. Gradually add the warmed milk and stir till smooth
6. Add the onion and allow to simmer for 30 min
7. Remove the onion and pass through a conical strainer
8. Cover with a film of butter to prevent a skin forming

MUSHROOM SAUCE

Ingredients

- 300 gm fresh or frozen mushrooms
- 1 tsp butter
- 2 shallots or 1 onion finely diced
- 200 gm crème fresh or double cream

Method

1 Heat the butter in a pan and add the onions, fry gently until they are soft and translucent
2 Add the mushrooms and cook for a further 5 min
3 Fold in the crème fresh or cream, bring to a simmer then season

PANCAKES

Ingredients

- ❖ 4 oz. flour of choice
- ❖ pinch of salt
- ❖ 1 egg
- ❖ ½ pt. milk
- ❖ ½ oz. melted butter or margarine
- ❖ 2 oz. castor sugar

Method

1. Sieve the flour and salt into a bowl, make a well in the centre
2. Add the egg and milk gradually, incorporating the flour from the side, whisk to a smooth batter
3. Mix the melted butter
4. Heat a pancake pan or small frying pan
5. Add a little oil, heat until smoking
6. Add enough batter to just cover the bottom of the pan thinly
7. Cook for a few seconds until brown
8. Turn over and cook the other side, turn onto a plate
9. Sprinkle with sugar, fold in half

Note: - can be filled with jam, apple puree or any other filling instead of the sugar

RATATOUILLE

Ingredients

- ❖ 8 oz. baby marrow
- ❖ 8 oz. aubergines
- ❖ 8 oz. tomatoes
- ❖ ⅛ pt. oil
- ❖ 2 oz. finely chopped onions
- ❖ 1 garlic clove peeled and chopped
- ❖ 2 oz. red pepper diced
- ❖ 2 oz. green pepper diced
- ❖ salt and pepper
- ❖ chopped parsley

Method

1 Trim off both ends of the marrow and aubergines
2 Remove skins of marrow and aubergines
3 Cut into 3mm (⅛ inch) slices
4 Concasse the tomatoes (peel, remove seeds, roughly chop)
5 Place oil in a thick bottomed pan and add onions
6 Cover with a lid and allow to cook gently for 5-7 min without colouring
7 Add the garlic, marrow aubergines and peppers
8 Season lightly with salt and pepper
9 Allow to cook gently for 4-5 min, toss occasionally and keep covered
10 Add the tomatoes and continue cooking for 20-30 min or until tender
11 Mix in the parsley, add salt and pepper to taste and serve
Note: - to concasse the tomatoes cut a cross in the bottom of tomatoes and
place in boiling water for 30 seconds until the skin begins to peel, remove and plunge into cold water, peel the skin off cut into 4 and remove seeds.

VEGAN BANANA BREAD

Ingredients

- ❖ 4 ripe bananas peeled
- ❖ 200 gm soft light brown sugar
- ❖ 100 gm vegetable oil
- ❖ 250 gm self-rising flour
- ❖ 50 gm ground almonds
- ❖ 1 tbsp. cinnamon
- ❖ icing sugar for dusting

Method

1 Line a 2lb loaf tin with baking parchment (or use a removable paper tray inside tin)
2 Mash 3 bananas in a large bowl, add the sugar and oil and mix thoroughly
3 Add the flour, ground almonds and cinnamon and stir to a smooth batter. If batter seems thick add a splash of dairy free milk to loosen
4 Pour into the loaf tin, then halve the remaining banana lengthways
5 Sit both halves on top of the mix cut side upwards
6 Bake for 1 hr at 180C until a skewer inserted into the middle comes out clean
7 Turn out onto a wire rack and allow to cool
8 Dust with icing sugar before slicing

WELSH RAREBIT

Ingredients

- 1 oz. butter or margarine
- ½ oz. flour
- ¼ pt. milk
- 4 oz. cheddar cheese
- 1 egg yoke
- 4 tbsp. beer
- salt, cayenne pepper, Worcester sauce (contains anchovies), English mustard (seasoning for personal flavour)

- ½ oz. butter or margarine
- slices of toast

Method

1 Melt 1oz. of butter/margarine in a thick based pan
2 Add the flour and mix with a wooden spoon
3 Cook on a gentle heat for a few min without colouring
4 Gradually add the milk and mix to a smooth paste
5 Add the grated cheese
6 Allow to melt slowly over a gentle heat until a smooth mixture is obtained
7 Add the yoke to the mixture, stir in well and remove from heat
8 Place the beer in a separate pan, bring to the boil and reduce to half a tablespoon
9 Add to the mixture with the other seasonings
10 Allow the mixture to cool
11 Spread onto the buttered toast
12 Place on a baking sheet and brown gently under the grill

Currys

"The Army is the true nobility of our country." – Napoleon Bonaparte

Positivi-tea

Sitting and enjoying a cup of tea is something often taken for granted. Try and make a cup of tea from start to finish, without moving onto another thing while the kettle boils. Sit and drink your cuppa and focus on the taste, if you take sugar, how sweet is it? If it's flavoured, have you tried a new flavour? Allowing yourself a break without thinking of other tasks can help clear and refocus your mind ready for the rest of the day. This doesn't have to be tea, any drink works!

CHICKEN TIKKA

Ingredients

- ❖ 3 lb Chicken, cut for sauté
- ❖ ½ pt. yoghurt
- ❖ 1tbsp grated ginger
- ❖ 1tbsp ground coriander
- ❖ 1 tbsp. ground cumin
- ❖ 1 tbsp. chilli powder
- ❖ 1 tbsp. chilli powder
- ❖ 1 clove of garlic chopped
- ❖ ½ lemon, juice of
- ❖ 2 oz. tomato puree
- ❖ 2 oz. onion finely chopped
- ❖ ⅛ pt. of oil
- ❖ 4 lemon wedges
- ❖ seasoning

Method

1   Place the chicken pieces in a suitable dish
2   Mix together the yoghurt, seasoning, spices, garlic, lemon juice and tomato puree
3   Pour this over the chicken, mix well and leave to marinade for at least 3 hrs
4   In a suitable shallow tray, add the chopped onion and half the oil
5   Lay the chicken pieces on top and grill, turning the pieces over once or gently cook in a moderate oven at 180C for 20–30 min
6   Baste with the remaining oil
7   Serve on a bed of lettuce garnished with the lemon wedges

CURRIED CHICKEN

Ingredients

- 2½ - 3 lb chicken
- 2 oz. oil
- 8 oz. onion
- 1 clove garlic
- ½ oz. flour
- ½ oz. curry powder
- 1 oz. tomato puree
- 1 pt. chicken stock
- 1 oz. sultanas
- 1 oz. chopped chutney
- ½ oz. desiccated coconut
- 2 oz. chopped apple
- ½ oz. root ginger or ¼ oz. ground ginger

Method

1 Cut the chicken as for sauté, season with salt and pepper
2 Heat the oil in a pan and add the chicken and lightly brown
3 Add the chopped onion and garlic
4 Cover pan with lid and cook gently for 3-4 min
5 Mix in the flour and curry powder
6 Mix in the tomato puree. Moisten with stock
7 Bring to the boil, skim
8 Add the remainder of ingredients, simmer until cooked
9 The sauce may be finished with 2 tbsp. cream or yogurt

DAHL

Ingredients

- ❖ 8 oz. lentils
- ❖ 1 tbsp. turmeric
- ❖ 2 oz. gee, butter or oil
- ❖ 2 oz. onion finely chopped
- ❖ 1 garlic clove crushed and chopped
- ❖ 1 green chilli finely chopped
- ❖ 1 tbsp. cumin seeds

Method

1 Place the lentils in a saucepan and cover with water.
2 Add the turmeric, bring to the boil and gently simmer until cooked. Stir occasionally
3 In a suitable pan, heat the fat and sweat the onion, garlic, chilli and cumin seeds. Stir into the lentils
4 Serve hot to accompany other dishes, the consistency should be fairly thick but not spoonable

Pasties
Pies

"This will remain the land of the free so long as it is the home of the brave." –Elmer Davis

Check-in

During the day, check-in with yourself. How does your body feel, are you tense or achy? If so, focus on relaxing it. If you feel your mind is wandering, try to focus on something and bring yourself back into the here and now.

BEEF PIE

Ingredients

- ❖ 1 lb prepared stewing beef (chuck rib)
- ❖ 2 oz. fat or oil
- ❖ 4 oz. onion chopped
- ❖ ¼ pint water, stock, red wine or beer
- ❖ salt pepper
- ❖ few drops of Worcester sauce
- ❖ 1 tsp chopped parsley
- ❖ ½ oz. cornflour
- ❖ 4 oz. short, puff or rough puff pastry

Method

1 Cut meat into 1 inch strips then into squares
2 Heat oil in a frying pan until smoking, add the meat and quickly brown on all sides
3 Drain the meat off in colander
4 Lightly fry the onions
5 Place the meat, onion, Worcester sauce, parsley and liquid into a pan, season lightly with salt and pepper
6 Bring to the boil, skim, then allow to simmer gently until meat is tender
7 Dilute the cornflour with a little water, stir into simmering mixture
Re-boil and add salt and pepper to taste
8 Place mixture into a pie dish and allow to cool
9 Cover with pastry, egg wash and bake at 200C for 30-45 min

Note: - this mix can be used to make individual pies or pasties

CHICKEN PIE

Ingredients

- ❖ 2½ -3 lb chicken
- ❖ salt pepper
- ❖ 4 oz. streaky bacon
- ❖ 4 oz. button mushrooms
- ❖ 1 chopped onion
- ❖ ½ pt. chicken stock
- ❖ pinch of chopped parsley
- ❖ 1 hard-boiled egg (chopped)
- ❖ 8 oz. puff pastry

Method

1 Cut the chicken into 1½ x ½ inch dice and season well with salt and pepper
2 Wrap each piece in very thin streaky bacon. Place in pie dish
3 Add the washed sliced mushrooms and remainder of ingredients
4 Add sufficient cold stock to barely cover the chicken
5 Cover and cook, bring to the boil and then simmer until cooked, allow 1-1½ hrs cooking
6 Cover with pastry and seal edges
7 Cook for a further 30-45 min until pastry is cooked
   Note: - mixture can be used without a pastry base or cooled and placed into   individual pie cases

CORNISH PASTY

Ingredients

- ❖ 8 oz. short pastry
- ❖ 4 oz. finely diced potato raw
- ❖ 4 oz. raw lamb or beef cut into small thin pieces
- ❖ 2 oz. chopped onion
- ❖ 2 oz. finely diced swede raw this is optional

Method

1 Roll out the short pastry 3mm (⅛ inch) thick and cut into 12cm rounds (5 inch)
2 Mix the remaining ingredients together, moisten with a little water and place in centre of round pastry, egg wash the edges
3 Fold in half and seal, flute the edges with a fork and egg wash
4 Cook in moderate oven at 150-200C for 45-60 min
5 A variety of fillings and seasoning can be used

MEAT AND VEG PASTIES

Ingredients

- ❖ Make a pastry of choice and wrap in cling film and place in fridge
- ❖ 2 large potatoes
- ❖ 2 carrots
- ❖ 1 tin of peas
- ❖ 8 oz. beef skirt or minced beef
- ❖ 1 egg
- ❖ salt and pepper to taste

Method

1 Peel and boil the potatoes and carrots for 5 min
2 Cut potatoes into small pieces same with the carrots
3 Cut the beef into same size as potatoes and carrots
4 Add all ingredients into a bowl and mix thoroughly, salt and pepper to taste
5 Roll out the pastry and cut to desired size (use a plate or saucer)
6 Add all ingredients into a bowl and mix thoroughly
7 Add required quantity of mix to centre of pastry round
8 Beat the egg and wet the outside of the pastry
9 Fold the pastry to make a ½ moon shape and press the edges down
10 Use a fork to crimp the edges and egg wash the pasties
11 Place on a baking tray and cook in a hot oven Gas Mark 6 or 400F for 30 min or until golden brown

SAUSAGE ROLLS

Ingredients

❖ 8 oz. puff pastry
❖ 1 lb sausage meat, (sausages could be used but remove meat from skin)

Method

1 Roll out the pastry to ⅛ inch thick into strips of 4 in wide
2 Make sausage meat into 1 in diameter
3 Place on pastry. Moisten the edge of the pastry
4 Fold over and seal, cut into 3 inch lengths
5 Use a knife or folk to seal the edges
6 Then brush with an egg
7 Place on a greased tray
8 Bake at 220C for about 20 min
    Note: - you can add apple finely diced to the meat as an alternative or buy specific sausages, i.e. wild boar, venison etc.

STEAK PUDDING

Ingredients

- ❖ 8 oz. suet paste
- ❖ 1 lb prepared stewing beef (chuck rib)
- ❖ Worcester sauce
- ❖ 1tsp chopped parsley
- ❖ salt and pepper
- ❖ 2-4 oz. chopped onion
- ❖ ¼ pint water

Method

1. Line a greased 1½ pt. basin with ¾ of the used paste and retain ¼ for the top
2. Mix all the other ingredients together
3. Place in the basin with the water to within ½ inch of the top
4. Moisten the edge of the suet paste, cover with the top and seal firmly
5. Cover with greased greaseproof paper and also, if possible, foil or pudding cloth securely tied with string
6. Cook in a steamer for 3½ hrs

Note: - add 2-4 oz. sheep's kidney or mushrooms if required

CHEESE AND ONION PIE / PASTY

Ingredients

- ❖ 1 large potatoes peeled and chopped into small pieces
- ❖ 1 medium onion sliced small
- ❖ 8 oz hard cheese of choice (cheddar, cathedral etc.)
- ❖ pastry from pastry recipe
- ❖ 4oz flour
- ❖ 1 or 2 tsp of mustard
- ❖ ½ to ¾ pt milk
- ❖ 2oz butter

Method

1. Dice and boil the potatoes
2. Cook the chopped onions in oil until soft but do not brown
3. Grate the cheese
4. Melt the butter then add the flour, stir to a thick paste, add the milk slowly bit by bit
5. And stir continually to bring back to a paste , add more milk and do the same
6. This should take 5 , 10 mins. You should end up with a smooth white sauce
7. Add the grated cheese and mustard to the sauce, this will thicken it slightly
8. Add the potatoes and onions to the sauce and stir to fully mix, do not over mix
9. Roll out your pastry and line a small pie dish .
10. Fill the pie dish with the mixture to ¼ inch from top
11. Add grated cheese to top of mix
12. Cook in oven 180c for 50 to 60 mins
13. For pasties roll out pastry and cut into circles or squares

NOTES:
for pasties - mash the potatoes and onions slowly add the sauce, when it is mixed but still firm let it cool and make your pasties
you can make the pastry following the instructions for short pastry
you can use any mustard of choice

Sweets

"A safe army is better than a safe border"- B.R. Ambedkar

Exercise

Exercising releases endorphins, the feel-good hormone in the brain. From running a marathon to a 5-minute stroll, exercising in any capacity contributes to mindfulness and improves mental health.

AFTERNOON TEA SCONES

Ingredients

- ❖ 8 oz. flour
- ❖ 1 ½ teaspoon baking powder
- ❖ ¼ teaspoon salt
- ❖ 1 egg
- ❖ 1oz. castor sugar
- ❖ 1 oz. margarine
- ❖ 1 oz. currants
- ❖ milk to mix

Method

1 Sieve the flour and salt and rub in the margarine
2 Add the dry ingredients
3 Add the egg and enough milk to make a soft dough
4 Turn out on a floured table or board, knead lightly to a smooth round ball
5 Roll out to ½ inch thick
6 Cut into rounds 12-16 scones
7 Bake on a greased baking tray and bake for 10 to 15 min Gas Mark 8 or 450 F

ANZAC BISCUITS

Ingredients

- ❖ 1 cup of wholemeal flour
- ❖ 1 cup of sugar
- ❖ 1 cup of desiccated coconut
- ❖ 125 gm porridge oats
- ❖ 1 tbsp. butter
- ❖ 2 tbsp. of golden syrup or treacle
- ❖ 2 tbsp. of boiling water
- ❖ 1tsp of bi-carbonate of soda

Method

1 Mix the flour, sugar and coconut together
2 Mix the syrup/treacle and butter together and warm gently until thoroughly mixed
3 Add the wet mixture into the dry mixture and bind together
4 Drop a tsp of mixture onto parchment paper lining a tray
5 Bake in oven at 180C until golden brown all over
6 Remove and leave to cool for 10 min before placing on a wire rack to finish cooling

APPLE CHARLOTTE

Ingredients

- ❖ 1 lb stale bread white or brown
- ❖ 4 oz. margarine or butter
- ❖ 1 lb cooking apples
- ❖ 2–3 oz. sugar castor or refined
- ❖ 1½ oz. bread crumbs or cake crumbs

Method

1. Use either 1 charlotte mould or 4 dariole moulds
2. Cut the bread into ⅛ slices and remove the crusts
3. Cut the round the size of the bottom of the mould, dip into melted butter or margarine on one side and place in mould fat side down
4. Cut fingers of bread 1-1½ inch wide and fit over lapping well, to the sides of the mould after dipping in melted fat - take care not to leave any gaps
5. Peel, core and wash the apples, cut into thick slices and 3-part cook in a little butter and sugar, and add the breadcrumbs
6. Fill the centre of the mould with the apple
7. Cut round pieces of bread to seal the apple in
8. Bake at 220C for 30-40 min, remove from the mould
9. Serve with custard, ice cream or cream

APPLE FLAN

Ingredients

- ❖ 4 oz. sugar paste
- ❖ 2 oz. sugar
- ❖ 1 lb cooking apples
- ❖ 2 tbsp. apricot glaze

Method

1. Line a flan dish with the sugar paste.
2. Keep the best shaped apples and make the remainder into a puree
3. When cool place in the flan dish
4. Peel quarter and wash the remaining apples
5. Cut into neat thin slices and lay carefully on the apple puree over lapping each slice. Ensure that each slice points to the centre of the flan then no difficulty should be encountered in joining the pattern up
6. Sprinkle a little sugar on the apple slices and bake the flan at 200C for 30-40 min
7. When flan is almost cooked, remove the flan ring carefully return to the oven to complete the cooking, mask with hot apricot glaze
   Note: - apricot glaze –boil apricot jam with a little water and pass through a strainer. Glaze should be used hot

BAKED EGG CUSTARD

Ingredients

- 3 small eggs
- sugar refined or castor
- 2-3 drops of vanilla essence
- 1 pt. milk whole or skimmed
- grated nutmeg

Method

1 Whisk the eggs, sugar and essence
2 Pour onto the warmed milk whisking continuously
3 Pass through a sieve into pie dish
4 Add a little grated nutmeg, wipe the edge of pie dish clean
5 Stand in a roasting tray half full of water and cook slowly in a moderate oven at 160C for 45 min to 1 hr

BREAD AND BUTTER PUDDING

Ingredients

- ❖ 1 oz. sultanas
- ❖ 2 slices of white or wholemeal bread, spread with butter or margarine
- ❖ 3 eggs
- ❖ 2 oz. sugar, caster or refined
- ❖ 2-3 drops vanilla essence
- ❖ 1 pt. milk whole or skimmed

Method

1 Wash the sultanas and place in pie dish
2 Remove the crust from the bread and cut each slice into 4 triangles neatly arrange overlapping in the pie dish
3 Prepare the egg custard (see baked egg custard)
4 Strain on into the bread dusting lightly with sugar
5 Cook and serve

BREAD PUDDING

Ingredients

- ❖ 1 lb stale white bread or wholemeal
- ❖ 5 oz. caster sugar
- ❖ 5 oz. currants or sultanas
- ❖ ½ tsp mixed spice
- ❖ 3 oz. margarine
- ❖ 1 egg

Method

1 Soak the bread in cold water until soft
2 Squeeze the bread dry and place in a bowl
3 Mix in four-fifths sugar and the rest of the ingredients
4 Place in a greased baking tray, sprinkle with remaining sugar
5 Bake tray 180C for about 1 hr

CHELSEA BUN

Ingredients

- ❖ butter or margarine
- ❖ 1 oz. currants
- ❖ 1 oz. sultanas
- ❖ 1 oz. chopped peel
- ❖ castor sugar

Method

1 Take a basic bun dough and roll out into a large square
2 Brush with melted butter or margarine
3 Sprinkle liberally with caster sugar
4 Sprinkle with the currants, sultanas and chopped peel
5 Roll up like a Swiss roll, brush with melted butter or margarine
6 Cut into slices across the roll (1½ in) wide
7 Place on a greased baking tray with deep sides
8 Cover and allow to prove
9 Bake in a hot oven at 220C for 15–20 min
10 Brush the buns with a bun wash as soon as cooked
   Note: - bun wash is ¼ lb of sugar and ½ pt. water brought to the boil until the consistency of a thick syrup

ECCLES CAKES

Ingredients

❖ 8 oz. rough or puff pastry

Filling
❖ 2 oz. butter or margarine
❖ 2 oz. mixed peel
❖ 2 oz. demerara sugar
❖ 8 oz. currants
❖ pinch of mixed spice

Method

1 Roll out the pastry 1½ inch thick
2 Cut into rounds, 4-5-inch diameter
3 Damp the edges with water
4 Place a tbsp. of the mixture in the centre of each ring
5 Fold the edges over to the centre and completely seal in the mixture
6 Brush the top with egg white and dip in castor sugar
7 Place on a greased baking tray
8 Cut 2 or 3 incisions with a knife so as to show the filling
9 Bake at 220C for 15–20 min

MANCHESTER TART

Ingredients

- shortcrust pastry
- 575 ml whole milk
- 3 tbsp. custard powder
- 3 tbsp. castor sugar
- 1 tbsp. vanilla essence
- 3 tbsp. raspberry jam (or jam of choice)
- 5 tbsp. desiccated coconut

Method

1 Roll out the pastry and line a tart case, prick the pastry with a fork
2 Place a sheet of baking parchment on the pastry and fill with baking beans
3 Bake for 20 min, at 200C, remove from oven and remove the beans and parchment
4 Replace in oven for 5 minutes, remove and leave to cool
5 Place the milk and sugar, custard powder and vanilla essence in a pan heat up gently, keep stirring until the mixture is smooth and thick (5–10 min)
6 Leave to cool (cover with a cartouche) to stop skin forming
7 Once everything is cool, spread the jam on the pastry base and sprinkle with ½ the coconut
8 Pour the custard over the jam and coconut and sprinkle the rest of the coconut on the custard, place in fridge to cool before serving

MINCE PIES

Ingredients

- ❖ 8 oz. puff pastry
- ❖ 8 oz. mince meat

Method

1 Roll out the pastry to ⅛ thick
2 Cut ½ the pastry into fluted rounds 2½ inch diameter
3 Place on a greased, dampened baking sheet
4 Moisten the edges
5 Place a little mincemeat in the centre of each
6 Cut the remainder of the pastry into fluted rounds 3-inch diameter
7 Cover the mincemeat and seal the edges
 Note: - you can use bought mincemeat in jars for this recipe

PARKIN

Ingredients

- ❖ 200 gm butter
- ❖ 1 egg
- ❖ 4 tbsp. golden syrup
- ❖ 85 gm treacle
- ❖ 1tbsp ground ginger
- ❖ 85 gm soft light brown sugar
- ❖ 100 gm medium oatmeal
- ❖ 250 gm self-rising flour

Method

1 Gently melt the syrup, treacle, sugar and butter in a pan until sugar is dissolved
2 Remove pan from heat
3 Mix the oatmeal, flour and ginger, stir into the syrup mix followed by the egg and milk, mix well
4 Pour the mixture into a 22cm square baking tin
5 Bake for 50-60 min at 160C until the top is crusty
6 Cool in the tin then wrap in parchment and tin foil until ready to eat
7 If kept for up to 5 days prior to eating the parkin will become soft and sticky
Note: - this is normally made for bonfire night but good at any time

ROCK CAKES

Ingredients

- 8 oz. flour
- ¼ oz. baking powder
- pinch of salt
- 3 oz. butter or margarine
- 3 oz. castor sugar
- 1 large egg
- 2 oz. dried fruit (currants, sultanas)

Method

1. Sieve the flour, baking powder and salt
2. Rub in the butter or margarine to a sandy mixture
3. Add the sugar
4. Gradually add the well beaten egg and mix lightly until combined
5. Place with a folk into 8 rough shapes on a greased baking tray
6. Milk or egg wash
7. Bake in a fairly hot oven at 220C for 20 min

SCONES

Ingredients

- ❖ 8 oz. self-rising flour
- ❖ ¼ oz. baking powder
- ❖ pinch of salt
- ❖ 2 oz. butter or margarine
- ❖ 2 oz. castor sugar
- ❖ 3/16 oz. milk or water

Method

1 Sieve the flour, baking powder and salt
2 Rub in the butter or margarine to a sandy texture
3 Make a well in the centre
4 Dissolve the sugar into the liquid
5 Gradually add to the flour mixture and mix lightly

6 Roll out on a floured surface to ½ in thick
7 Cut into rounds size required
8 Place on a greased baking tray and milk wash and bake at 200C for 15–20 min
Note: - cheese or sultanas can be added to the mix prior to rolling out

SHORTBREAD

Ingredients

- 6 oz. soft flour
- pinch of salt
- 4 oz. butter or margarine
- 2 oz. castor sugar

Method

1 Sift the flour and salt
2 Mix in the butter or margarine and sugar with the flour
3 Combine all ingredients to a smooth paste
4 Roll out carefully on a floured surface to the shape of a rectangle or round to ¼ inch thick
5 Place on a greased baking tray
6 Mark into desired size and shape, prick with a fork
7 Bake in a moderate oven at 180–200C for 15–20 min
Note: - the mixture can be placed into a shallow baking tin (½ inch deep if required)

Cakes

"The veterans of our military services have put their lives on the line to protect the freedoms that we enjoy. They have dedicated their lives to their country and deserve to be recognized for their commitment." – Judd Greg

Slow down

Slowing down and becoming aware of the journey allows your mind to relax so that the next task or step of your day is done in a calm and productive manner.

Close your eyes

Closing your eyes for a couple of minutes throughout the day helps to clear your mind and avoid distractions while looking at things so you can refocus your attention elsewhere.

CHRISTMAS CAKE

Ingredients

- ❖ 1 lb butter or margarine
- ❖ 1 lb demerara sugar
- ❖ 10 eggs
- ❖ 2 tbsp. mixed spice
- ❖ 1 lb currants
- ❖ 8 oz. raisins
- ❖ 4 oz. glazed cherries
- ❖ 1 lb sultanas
- ❖ 8 oz. mixed peel
- ❖ glass of brandy or rum
- ❖ 2 tbsp. glycerine
- ❖ 4 oz. chopped almonds
- ❖ 1½ lb soft flour

Method

1 Cream the butter and sugar until light and fluffy
2 Gradually beat in the eggs, creaming continually
3 Mix in the spice, brandy or rum, glycerine and chopped almonds
4 Fold in the ground almonds and flour
5 Correct the consistency with milk if necessary
6 Line a 10-12 inch cake tin with silicone paper
7 Add the mixture, spread evenly
8 Bake at 160C for 1½ hrs
9 Reduce the heat to 150C for 1½ hrs
10 Reduce the heat to 140C for 30–60 min or until cooked
11 Insert a skewer into the centre of cake when cooked it should come out clean and free of uncooked mixture
12 Remove from oven, allow to set for 15 min, then remove from tin and allow to cool

Note: - decorating cake
   Brush with boiling apricot jam, cover sides and top with marzipan and finally   coat with icing sugar and decorate

GENOESE SPONGE

Ingredients

- ❖ 4 eggs
- ❖ 4 oz. castor sugar
- ❖ 4 oz. soft flour
- ❖ 2 oz. butter or margarine

Method

1. Whisk the eggs and sugar with a balloon whisk in a bowl over a pan of hot water
2. Continue until the mixture is light, creamy and doubled in bulk
3. Remove from the heat and whisk until cold and thick
4. Fold in the flour very gently
5. Fold in the melted butter very gently
6. Place in a greased floured Genoese mould
7. Bake in a moderately hot oven at 200-220C for approx. 30 min

SMALL CAKES

Ingredients

- ❖ 8 oz. soft flour
- ❖ 1 level spoon of baking powder
- ❖ salt
- ❖ 5 oz. butter or margarine
- ❖ 5 oz. castor sugar
- ❖ 2-3 eggs

Method

1. Sieve the flour, baking powder and salt
2. Rub in the butter or margarine to a sandy texture
3. Add the sugar
4. Gradually add the beaten eggs and mix as lightly as possible until combined

Note: - the consistency should be a light dropping one.
Cherry cake: add 2 oz. glazed chopped cherries
    Coconut cake: in place of 2 oz. of flour add 2 oz. desiccated coconut

VICTORIA SANDWICH

Ingredients

- ❖ 4 oz. butter or margarine
- ❖ 4 oz. castor sugar
- ❖ 2 eggs
- ❖ 4 oz. soft flour
- ❖ ¼ oz. baking powder

Method

1. Cream the fat and sugar until soft and fluffy
2. Gradually add the beaten eggs
3. Lightly mix in the sieved flour and baking powder
4. Divide into two 7-inch greased sponge tins
5. Bake at 190-200C for 12-15 min
6. Turn out onto a wire rack to cool
7. Spread one half with jam, place the other half on top
8. Dust with icing sugar
   Note: - for chocolate sandwich use 3 oz. flour and 1 oz. cocoa powder

Pastry

"On the battlefield, the military pledges to leave no soldier behind. As a nation, let it be our pledge that when they return home, we leave no veteran behind." – Dan Lipinski

Doodles

Doodling is a quick and easy stress relief to take a few minutes out focussing on something light-hearted. Scrap piece of paper or a dedicated doodle pad, all surfaces work for this activity, and afterwards you have a clear mind to go forward.

Grounding

During stressful or overwhelming situation, grounding yourself can be an excellent way to refocus the mind. Sit with your hands in fists on your legs, eyes closed. Focus on a happy memory, where it was, who was there, what was happening around you? Focussing on these things and revisiting a happy memory grounds the mind in a positive state so you are better able to go on with the day in a positive mind-set.

BUN DOUGH

Ingredients

- ❖ ½ lb strong flour
- ❖ ¼ oz. yeast
- ❖ ⅛ pt. milk and water
- ❖ 1 egg
- ❖ 2 oz. butter or margarine
- ❖ 1 oz. castor sugar

Method

1 Sieve the flour into a warm bowl
2 Cream the yeast in a basin with a little liquid
3 Make a well in the centre of the flour
4 Add the dispersed yeast, sprinkle with a little flour, cover with a cloth and leave in a warm place until the yeast ferments (bubbles)
5 Add the beaten egg, butter or margarine, sugar and remainder of liquid knead well to form a soft, slack dough, knead until smooth and free from stickiness
6 Keep covered and allow to prove in a warm place
7 Use as required

CHOUX PASTRY

Ingredients

- ❖ 2 oz. flour
- ❖ 2 oz. butter or margarine
- ❖ 5 fluid oz. water
- ❖ pinch of salt
- ❖ few drops of vanilla
- ❖ 2 eggs

Method

1. Sieve the flour
2. Put the water, fat and salt in a small saucepan and bring to boiling point
3. Draw pan aside and add flour at once
4. Beat in the flour till smooth over gentle heat
5. When cool, add vanilla essence and beat in eggs one at a time very thoroughly
6. To make eclairs (10–12)
   pipe the mixture in rolls on greased tin, using a ⅓-inch plain pipe nozzle
7. Bake in a hot oven for 30 min till crisp and light coloured gas mark 6 or 400F.
   Avoid draughts throughout cooking
8. When baked, split the eclairs at one side and cool them on a rack
9. Fill with sweetened and flavoured cream
10. Ice the top with chocolate icing

FLAKY PASTRY

Ingredients

- ❖ ¾ fat to flour
- ❖ 2 teaspoon lemon juice to each ½ lb flour
- ❖ 5 fluid oz. water to each ½ lb flour
- ❖ ¼ teaspoon salt to each ½ lb flour

Method

1 Divide the fat into four pieces and keep it cool
2 Aerate the flour and salt with fingers
3 Rub ¼ of fat into the flour and mix to a soft dough with the cold water and lemon juice added all at once
4 Leave to relax for 30 min
5 Knead very lightly and roll into a strip
6 Spread another ¼ fat in tiny parts over ⅔ of the strip
7 Fold the pastry in three, with the plain ⅓ inside, seal the edges and half turn the pastry
8 Repeat steps 5 and 7 twice, then roll and fold without the fat being enclosed
9 When the pastry has been rolled and folded 4 times, roll it to the required size
10 Bake at gas mark 7 or 430F

ROUGH PUFF PASTRY

Ingredients

- ❖ 8 oz. flour
- ❖ 5-6 oz. fat
- ❖ ½ teaspoon of salt
- ❖ cold water
- ❖ 2 teaspoon of lemon juice

Method

1 Sieve the flour and salt into a dry bowl
2 Add the fat cut into square pieces the size of walnuts
3 Add the lemon juice and cold water to bind to a soft dough,
4 But do not break down the fat
5 Turn out onto a floured surface or board and lightly press the pastry together but do not knead it
6 Roll out to a strip keeping sides even and ends square
7 Fold the pastry in three
8 Seal the edges with rolling pin
9 Half turn pastry and bring the folded edges to the side
10 Roll out to a strip, being careful to avoid rolling over the top and bottom edges as this will expel the air folded into the pastry
11 Repeat rolling and turning the pastry till it has four rolls and turns
12 Roll out the pastry to size and thickness required
13 Bake in hot oven at gas mark 7 or 430F

SHORT PASTRY

<u>Ingredients</u>

- ❖ ½ to ⅓ fat to flour
- ❖ cold water to bind
- ❖ 1 tea spoon salt to each lb of flour
- ❖ for richer pastry, 1 egg yolk to each ½ lb flour

Note: - if fat is used, add 1 teaspoon of baking powder to each 1 lb of flour

<u>Method</u>

1. Sieve the flour and salt into a dry cool bowl
2. Rub the fat into the flour with the tips of your fingers until the mixture resembles fine breadcrumbs
3. Add sufficient water or egg yolk and water to form a stiff dough
4. Turn the dough out onto a floured surface or board, and knead slightly until it is free from cracks
5. Then roll it out to the size required. The dough should be about 1/8th of an inch thick.
6. Bake in a hot oven gas mark 6 or 400 F

SUET PASTRY

Ingredients

- ½ to ⅓ suet to flour
- 2 teaspoons of baking powder to each lb of flour
- cold water to bind
- 1 teaspoon of salt to each lb of flour

Method

1   Sieve the flour and salt into dry bowl
2   Shred and chop the suet with some flour
3   Mix the suet and flour, add the baking powder
4   Add water and mix till the ingredients are bound together and leave the bowl clean. The dough should be firm
5   Turn out onto a clean table or board, knead till free of cracks
6   Turn the smooth side up and roll out as required
7   Boil or steam quickly and steadily or bake in a hot oven

SUGAR PASTRY

Ingredients

- ❖ 1 egg
- ❖ 2 oz. sugar
- ❖ 5 oz. butter or margarine
- ❖ 8 oz. soft flour
- ❖ pinch of salt

Method

1 Taking care not to over soften, cream the egg and sugar
2 Add the butter or margarine and mix for a few seconds
3 Gradually add the sieved flour and salt
4 Mix lightly until smooth
5 Allow to rest in a cool place before using

Specials

"How important it is for us to recognize and celebrate our heroes and she-roes!" – Maya Angelou

> *"The pessimist complains about the wind; the optimist expects it to change; the realist adjusts the sails."* – William Arthur Ward

> *"A ship without Marines is like a garment without buttons."* – Admiral David D. Porter

EGG BANJO (for one)

**Recommended by the Bridge for Heroes Patron
General the Lord Dannatt GCB, CBE, MC, DL**

Ingredients

* 1 egg
* 2 thick slices of white or brown bread
* butter
* 1 tsp oil

Method

1   Heat the oil in a pan
2   Butter the two slices of bread thickly
3   When the oil is beginning to bubble turn the heat down and
    crack the egg into the pan. Spoon some of the fat over the
    yolk of the egg to help cook the top side but avoid over
    cooking.
4   Place the egg onto one of the slices of bread and place the
    second piece on top to make a sandwich

Note: - When biting into the sandwich the runny yolk may drip out
onto your top. Hold the sandwich at shoulder height in one hand
and with your other hand wipe any yolk from your top, in an up
and down motion! Like you are playing the Banjo!

SMOKED MACKEREL PATE (for four)

**A very quick but delicious recipe from
The Lady Dannatt MBE, HM Lord-Lieutenant of Norfolk**

Ingredients

- ❖ 1 pack of 2 smoked mackerel fillets, skin removed
- ❖ small pack of cheapest cream cheese (Philly type)
- ❖ juice of lemon
- ❖ black pepper
- ❖ dollop of crème fraiche or cream (optional)
- ❖ 1 teaspoonful horseradish sauce (optional)
- ❖ 2 oz. melted butter

Method

1   Combine together in a food processor or mash by hand.

Note: - Serve with brown toast, melba toast or anything else you prefer

And hey presto!

Note:- Salmon can be used instead of Mackerel

LOADED POT' (potato)

<u>Ingredients</u>

- ❖ 1 large potato
- ❖ 2 slices of bacon cut/chopped into small pieces
- ❖ 25g + 5g grated cheese
- ❖ 1 tsp olive oil
- ❖ Salt

<u>Method</u>

1   Pre heat the oven to 220C
2   Scrub clean the potato and prick a number of times with a folk
3   Heat on high in the microwave for between 12-14 min turning over half way through (reduce the time for a smaller potato)
4   Using a clean tea towel place the potato on a baking tray
5   Mix oil and salt together and rub/brush all over the potato
6   Place in the pre heated oven for further 20 minutes or until the skin is crispy and oven bake the bacon on a separate baking tray at the same time
7   Take out the cooked potato and bacon. Holding the potato in the tea towel, cut in half, then scoop out the potato from its 'jacket' into a bowl, being careful not to split the skins
8   Mash the potato and mix in the bacon and grated cheese
9   Spoon the mix back into the jackets and top with grated cheese
10 Place back in the oven for a further 10 min or until the grated cheese has melted and begun to brown slightly

Mindfulness

The little things? The little moments? They aren't little. -- Jon Kabat-Zinn

Meditation is not evasion; it is a serene encounter with reality. -- Thích Nhất Hạnh

When we get too caught up in the busyness of the world, we lose connection with one another – and ourselves. -- Jack Kornfield

Nothing ever goes away until it has taught us what we need to know. -- Pema Chödrön

Mindfulness isn't difficult, we just need to remember to do it. -- Sharon Salzberg

That's life: starting over, one breath at a time. -- Sharon Salzberg

Don't believe everything you think. Thoughts are just that – thoughts. -- Allan Lokos

There is something wonderfully bold and liberating about saying yes to our entire imperfect and messy life. -- Tara Brach

Looking at beauty in the world, is the first step of purifying the mind. -- Amit Ray

A few simple tips for life: feet on the ground, head to the skies, heart open...quiet mind. -- Rasheed Ogunlaru

If the problem can be solved why worry? If the problem cannot be solved worrying will do you no good. – Buddha

Do not dwell in the past, do not dream of the future, concentrate the mind on the present moment. – Buddha

The mind is just like a muscle – the more you exercise it, the stronger it gets and the more it can expand. -- Idowu Koyenikan

Mindful eating

Mindful eating means simply eating or drinking while being aware of each bite or sip. -- Thích Nhất Hạnh

Instead of thinking of food as the enemy, allow yourself to enjoy the process of planning and preparing meals or going out to lunch with a friend. Stay in the present moment and understand that the purpose of food is nourishment. -- Susan Albers

Mindful eating is about awareness. When you eat mindfully, you slow down, pay attention to the food you're eating, and savour every bite. -- Susan Albers

When you bow, you should just bow; when you sit, you should just sit; when you eat, you should just eat. -- Shunryu Suzuki

When I'm hungry, I eat what I love. When I'm bored, I do something I love. When I'm lonely, I connect with someone I love. When I feel sad, I remember that I am loved. -- Michelle May

GLOSSARY

Add **salt and pepper** to taste – 1 teaspoon salt & ½ teaspoon pepper – or more or less depending on your own preference

Bechamel – Classic French white sauce, used as the basis for other sauces and savoury dishes

Bind – mix beaten egg or other liquid into a dry mixture to help hold it together

Blanch – to immerse food briefly in fast-boiling water to loosen skins, such as tomatoes or to preserve flavour and colour

Bouquet garni – purchase from a supermarket. A tea bag full of herbs

Cartouche - parchment-paper lid

Concasse – Diced fresh ingredients, used as a garnish e.g. skinned, deseeded tomatoes

Conical (strainer) – small cone shape strainer

Cream – beat together fat and sugar until the mixture is light and fluffy, resembling whipped cream in texture and colour

Crème fraiche – a thick cultured cream soured with bacterial culture giving a nutty, tangy, slightly sour flour

Dariole – French term meaning a small truncated cone shaped mould

Dice – to cut food into small cubes

Dollop – A small amount of a soft food item, such as cream, that can be formed into a small round shape as a serving.

Knead – work dough by pummelling with the heel of your hand

Marinate – soak a mixture in meat to soften and impart flavour

Pate – a savoury mixture of finely chopped meat/fish/vegetables, usually served as a starter

Patty - flattened, usually round, serving of ground meat fish, grains, vegetables, or meat alternatives

Paysanne – cut your vegetables thinly but in the form of the vegetable being cut e.g. carrots cut very thinly but with varying sizes of circles

Prove – leave to rise after shaping

Sauté – cook food in a small quantity of fat over a high heat, shaking the pan constantly Sandy texture – grainy look like wet sand

Simmer – keep a liquid just below boiling point

Skim – remove froth or fat from the surface of stock, gravy etc. Use a skimmer or spoon

Stir fry – cook small evenly-sized pieces of food rapidly in a little fat, tossing constantly over a high heat

Whisk – beat air rapidly into a mixture

INDEX

www.ingramcontent.com/pod-product-compliance
Lightning Source LLC
Chambersburg PA
CBHW072042040426
42447CB00012BB/2979